MW01142348

Chastity

The Mystery of
Human Sexuality

Ann Nerbun & Mary Ann Fey

ONE LIGUORI DRIVE, LIGUORI, MO, 63057-9999

Imprimi Potest:
Richard Thibodeau, C.Ss.R.
Provincial, Denver Province
The Redemptorists

Imprimatur:
Most Reverend Michael J. Sheridan
Auxiliary Bishop, Archdiocese of St. Louis

ISBN 0-7648-0606-8
Library of Congress Catalog Card Number: 99-67979

Liguori Lifespan is an imprint of Liguori Publications.

To order, call 1-800-325-9521
http://www.liguori.org

Cover design by Wendy Barnes

Table of Contents

Introduction

Who Can Be Holy?

Who of us has not—at some point—wondered, who can be holy? A young daughter once said: "It's too hard to be good." A teenage son, desperately seeking approval, in a moment of self-pity, yelled: "You should just shoot me." How often a parent is brought to his or her knees, "Lord, I have failed again to bring peace and joy to my family."

Try as we might, holiness seems beyond our grasp. But to neglect our longing to be holy is to deny our humanity, and, therefore, a sin of omission. We may not be doing awful things, but we can easily forget God, separate ourselves from God's love, and deny the very essence of the Christian life, which is the pursuit of perfection (see Matthew 5:48). When we struggle to be holy, we dare to become fully human.

Do We Live in Vain?

Has God made us in the divine image only to make it impossible for us to become god-like? Are we not capable of loving as God loves? If that is how it is, then life is just a cruel hoax, a sham, a frustrating, hopeless journey destined for unfulfillment. We know that cannot be so. Because we believe in God's great love for us, we know that Christ, the Son of God, came into the world to redeem us—"to heal sinners"—and to show us how to love.

If I Have Not Love, I Am Nothing

As God's beloved sons and daughters—when we add our efforts to divine grace—we can achieve the fullness of Christian maturity and perfection. Saint Paul reminded the Corinthians that while there are many members in the one body, many gifts to be perfected, he would show them a "still more excellent way"

(1 Corinthians 12:31). To dedicate oneself to the excellent way is to love as Christ loves.

An Obstacle to the Good Life

Each age and culture presents particular obstacles to growth in the "excellent way" of holiness. Among the many obstacles in our age, is the incredible difficulty of growing in the virtue of chastity because the true meaning of human sexuality has been distorted almost beyond recognition. Mantras such as "Just do it" and "Have it your way" indicate how sexual love has been trivialized and reduced to immediate gratification of our senses, and "sex"—genital activity—has been elevated to godlike status. Yet, people are not toys: Unchaste behavior is uncharitable (non-loving), and stifles our efforts to become holy.

Everyone's Talking Sex

Everyone is talking about sex, but there is very little serious study or helpful conversation about what it truly means to be a sexual person. Surrounded by sexual messages and images in the media that portray unfaithfulness in marriage, promiscuity, cohabitation, and a host of aberrant sexual behaviors as normative, many men and women are left wondering how they can fulfill their true nature and deepest yearnings. Sexuality and sexual love have been stripped of the joy, hope, and peace that God intends for us even in this life. As part of our human nature, there is written in our soul a longing to share fully in God's love, and to fulfill the divine plan for the proper use of our sexual powers. Yet, it is almost as if we are being held hostage to cultural mores which continually dupe us to "look for love in all the wrong places."

What About These Teenagers Today?

"Oh my gosh, we have a problem!" Government, educators, politicians, sociologists, church leaders, and many parents are all openly concerned about the rate of adolescent pregnancy and sexually transmitted diseases, and are shocked by reports of teen sex rings, sexual brutality, and sadomasochistic behaviors. Much energy has been exerted to control the behavior, manage the crisis, and deal with the fallout. However, there has been little effort to understand the sexual person, human sexuality, and the mystery of marriage. It is important to understand that the prevailing expression of sexuality by adolescents is only a reflection of the profound confusion of adults concerning love and sexuality.

As young people mature, they learn by example. Therefore, the responsibility for clearing up the confusion about sex rightly rests with adults examining and coming to a proper understanding of the meaning of love and sexuality. Only then can chastity be proposed as a mark of fully integrated sexual persons capable of Christlike love in their relationships with others.

What Questions Need to Be Answered?

- What does it mean to be a sexual person?
- How can I integrate my life's purpose—to love—with my sexuality?
- What is the meaning of sexual intercourse?
- How does a virtuous life make for a good life?
- What is chastity?
- What does chastity have to do with love?
- How is chastity relevant to my life?
- Why is chastity a virtue for everyone?
- How will chastity affect my relationship with God?
- What does it take to live out the virtue of chastity in everyday life?

This booklet is the result of many years of reflecting on these questions. We, the authors, have gradually grown in our own appreciation of the incredible gift of sexuality. While imperfect in our understanding, we have become passionate in our desire to share with others in a realistic way the significance of chastity in the lifelong pursuit of living as a wholly sexual person before God.

Pope John Paul II has reminded us, time and again, that true sexual love is a gift from God integral to the divine plan for the union of man and woman in marriage. Mother Teresa talked about chastity as "self-control out of love for each other" (Mother Teresa's address at the National Prayer Breakfast, Feb. 3, 1994), and she is frequently remembered for saying that everyone is called to be a saint.

It is our hope that this booklet will be an inspiration for many to reflect on the mystery of being made sexual images of God, and so—in some small way—help each of us to become more holy. We know this is just a beginning for most of us. But as more people address their sexuality as a gift, and chastity as a central dimension of the freedom to live this truth, perhaps we will experience a second and more powerful sexual revolution.

We Are Sexual Persons

God created humankind in his image,
in the image of God he created them;
male and female he created them.

GENESIS 1:27

There is a book entitled, *Did Adam and Eve Have Belly Buttons? And 199 Other Questions From Catholic Teenagers* (by Matthew J. Pinto, Ascension Press, 1998). Back in the seventies, the great epic story *Roots* was made into a movie. Genealogy—tracing our ancestry—has captivated many aspiring family historians. Did you ever notice that a child never tires of hearing about his or her beginnings?

To understand and appreciate who we are as sexual persons, we need to go back to our "roots," our beginnings. Interestingly enough, three of the major world religions (Christianity, Judaism, and Islam) accept the Book of

Genesis as foundational to their belief system. The story of creation marks the beginning of almost every catechetical series. Socrates and Aristotle probably weren't the first ones to pose the questions, "Who am I? Where have I come from? What is my purpose in life?"

Rooted in Love

It was God's love and goodness that inspired all of creation. Genesis tells us that, of everything God created, only man and woman are made in the image and likeness of God. In "being man" and "being woman," we reflect the goodness of God's infinite perfection. Together, we reflect the fullness of God's love in the world. God's will in creating us as sexual beings touches every aspect of our existence as persons. It is body and soul deep: Sexuality is at the essence of who we are and what we do.

Our Bodies Are Not a Suit of Clothes

God created us as embodied persons, not as bodies without souls nor as souls without bodies. We don't get up in the morning and put on our bodies like a suit of clothes. God did not make a soul and wrap a body around it. Nor could we relate as persons without our bodies. We are so united in body and spirit that it is awkward, if not impossible, to describe one without the other. "Every sound in the soul echoes in the body, and every sound in the body echoes in the soul" (Peter Kreeft, *Everything You Wanted to Know About Heaven—But Never Dreamed of Asking*, Ignatius Press, 1997).

Not a Body Without a Soul

Imagine if someone were to come up and pinch you on the arm. Would you respond: "Ouch, you pinched my body! You hurt my body!"? Probably not. It would be much more natural and likely for you to exclaim: "Ouch, You pinched *me*; you hurt *me!*"

Nor a Soul Without a Body

On the other hand, it would be unusual for us to talk about our souls as if they were a separate part of who we are in our existence, "like a ghost in a machine" (Kreeft). We wouldn't say: "My mind does not believe this, so my will won't do it." No! We would say: "*I* do not believe, so *I* won't do it." In truth, our soul (our mind and will) defines us as human persons, as images of God. We express ourselves— and we invite others to know us—through our bodies, and each word or act is a demonstration of our thoughts, beliefs, and choices in life. Our bodies express the unique person we are. That is why it can be said we are embodied persons.

Sexuality Is Soul Deep

To be a person is to be sexual, in body and in soul. In fact, the most pervasive quality of being human is that we are sexual persons. Man and woman share a common soul as images of God, but with different manifestations. Our sexuality is everything in body, mind, and spirit that radiates from being male or female. In fact, we were conceived, born, live, and will die and exist eternally as a masculine or feminine person.

Our maleness or femaleness is at the core and center of who we are and our total response to all of life. It was trendy in the seventies and eighties to diminish the differences between male and female children. We gave our girls trucks and guns and our boys dolls and purses, convinced that gender differences were a result of cultural bias. We are now more free to acknowledge the goodness in the differences of masculine and feminine persons. Men *do* tend to be more analytical, sensual, task oriented, playful, and aggressive. Women *are* often more relational, emotional, sensitive, tender, and nurturing. Because God chose to make us equal and complementary, sexual integrity, the perfection of both the masculine and feminine dimensions of human persons, is essential if God is to be fully imaged in this world.

Called to Perfection as Sexual Beings

To image the fullness of God is to bring out the best in each other, to complete one another as masculine and feminine dimensions of the one God. We are called to respect the equality and reverence the "genius" of each gender. (Who but God would have thought up such an intriguing creative plan!) Our differences are very good, and it is right to appreciate—be fascinated by and attracted to—the mystery of being different. This appreciation for the differences was first expressed by Adam: "This at last is bone of my bones and flesh of my flesh"

(Genesis 2:23), and is repeated every time an adolescent reaches puberty!

God takes pleasure in our delight in the truth that man is made for woman and woman for man: "It is not good that the man should be alone" (Genesis 2:18). In wisdom and goodness, God not only made us male and female, but made each person multidimensional in his or her being, with different aspects that make up each masculine and feminine person.

The "SPICE" of Life

Each of us has *Spiritual, Physical, Intellectual, Creative, and Emotional* dimensions. We can call these the "SPICE" of life, because it is the development and maturation of each of these personal aspects that makes life so incredibly rich. To be fully expressive in imaging God means, first, that we each develop ourselves in our totality as sexual persons. We could compare this effort at self-development to athletes preparing for the decathlon. They have to strengthen and develop many different muscles and athletic skills to be fully ready. In the same way, each person has to develop all the dimensions of his/her personhood (SPICE) to become fully mature.

Acting as a Reflection of God

We can reflect God in a variety of ways through the dimensions of our personhood. We mirror God's orderliness through exercising intellect, the ability to solve problems, and the creativity to be good managers. Using our physical strength and emotional passion for a cause, such as to help build homes for the poor, can be a sharing of God's merciful compassion. Being open to sharing our personal life and faith journey with others may strengthen their own relationship with God. Indeed, the expression of who we are has the potential to make the presence and glory of God felt by others.

Fashioning One's Unique Gift

Sexual integrity is the integration of these SPICE dimensions. Our sexuality is the whole picture—not just body parts and functions—of who we are as totally sexual persons. What God wants us to do is "fashion a gift." We have been uniquely and wonderfully made, a "special order" unlike anyone else in time. No one else can image God in this world quite the way each one of us can. Through love and grace, God works with each one of us to become a beautiful someone, the very best masculine and feminine self. Thus, to be a great "lover" is to accept myself as "gift," and to choose to give the gift of myself totally to God and others.

Chastity Is Indispensable to Perfecting the "Gift"

Our sexuality is inseparable from our humanity. To be perfected in our humanity, we must be perfected in our sexuality. Chastity—

whether in a married or unmarried context—perfects our sexuality and is therefore indispensable to the refining perfection of our humanity. "Blessed are the pure in heart, for they will see God" (Matthew 5:8). We all have a vocation—a call—to see God. It is through our human relationships—both sexual and chaste—that we come to see God.

Sex Is About Relationships

"Sexuality...becomes personal and truly human when it is integrated into the relationship of one person to another" (*Catechism of the Catholic Church* [CCC], 2337), no matter one's state of life. Celibate and married love are the two forms in which a person's call to love is fulfilled. Each is valued and dignified insofar as the goodness of the other is recognized and upheld. In either state of life, sexual feelings should not be repressed or denied, but sexual energy should be rightly directed.

In marriage, sexual energy is directed toward

the bonding of the commitment which establishes the marriage relationship in mutual love. For the celibate or virgin, sexual energy is expressed through worthy acts directed to the good of others "for the sake of the Kingdom" and the glory of God. Chastity insures the integrity of us as sexual persons and should be "cultivated in the way that is suited to their way of life" (CCC 2349).

Chastity Nurtures Marital Love

As male and female, we are made for one another in a way to be uniquely expressed through marital love. Marital love ought to reflect a deep union of heart and soul... spiritually, physically, intellectually, creatively, and emotionally. A couple united in Christ stand together and look outside themselves to glorify God in their completion of the divine plan. Human sexuality has a special God-given place for its expression in marriage: husband and wife, bonded together—giving of themselves completely, freely, and permanently—to share with one another the love that God has shared with them, a love the benefits of which "overflows" to others.

The greatest moment in the life of a married couple is when they call into being a new life: a new image of God who will forever change the world and who will live eternally. Out of this love, man for woman, woman for man, bonded in holy marriage, the human family is born, reflecting the creative love between the Father, the Son, and the Holy Spirit.

REMEMBER:

We are wholly sexual persons, body and soul, male and female images of God. Our sexuality is who we are, not what we do. As sexual persons, we are created good, meant to be held in honor, to become perfect, and to bring glory to God.

Created to Love

I give you a new commandment, that you
love one another. Just as I have loved you,
you also should love one another.

JOHN 13:34

"Humanity is loved by God!" (John Paul II,
Christifidelis Laici, 34). The story of our
beginning is a story of love. In Genesis the
inspired author repeats over and over that God
saw that it was good: "God saw everything that
he had made, and indeed, it was very good"
(Genesis 1:31). Through the words of the
inspired author, we see God's total and abso-
lute delight in creation. Knowing the inherent
goodness of creation, we know that God cannot *not* love us. In this truth is our dignity and
purpose in life. We are not made merely for ourselves; we are not the purpose of our existence. It
is God's love that completes our life; each one

of us is made to share in God's own life and love.

Love Perfected

God's self-revelation stirs us to freely respond to this love by loving far beyond what we think is our natural capacity. "Love therefore is the fundamental and innate vocation of every human being" (John Paul II, *Familiaris Consortio*, 11). We begin by being created in love, and through the whole of our earthly existence we are drawn to completion and perfection in union with God who is Love. God does not command the impossible. God, the perfect Lover, wants nothing less than perfect love, peace, and deep abiding joy for us.

Human Love Is a Beautiful Thing

Our language can limit our understanding of love. The fact that we only have one word for "love" makes it difficult to distinguish between godlike love and a feeling or attraction to someone or something. We say: "I love… chocolate, a beautiful sunset, my mother." These expressions say that we recognize the beauty and goodness in all God has made for us. God has placed in us a desire or passion for that which can bring us happiness or pleasure.

This emotional expression of love begins with the self and ends with the self. It is not a conscious decision; it is by nature inscribed in our humanity to love what is good and beautiful and what satisfies our personal needs. But this kind of love won't hold up when there is nothing in it for me, or when I no longer find delight in the other. How predictable it is that a husband or wife will face the moment of doubt when the passion and enthusiasm of the honeymoon experience fades. What parent has not endured the reality that being Mom or Dad isn't always a warm, fuzzy feeling? Who has not put up with the foibles of a friend? God placed this need for emotional love in us ultimately to draw us to him. In this way, emotional love is important to our capacity to love as Christ loves, but by itself it is incomplete or imperfect love.

What Is Godlike Love?

Thank God, we are given a supernatural capacity to perfect our love by directing it toward a giving of self in union and friendship with God and others. We are to use things, but love persons. In fact, freely loving another is the exact opposite of using him or her. Such love is relational and "willed" in that it requires the use of our mind and will. It must be a conscious choice and a free act. As a reflection of God, willed love is generous and desires only what is best for God, for oneself, and for all other persons that God has created.

If we truly love God, we desire to work to bring God's love into the world. Willed love is directed toward others—who are images of God—and fosters a communion of persons.

This expression of love is a decision to focus on giving the "gift of self" rather than seeking pleasure or happiness for myself. Such love compassionately nurses a sick and whining child, cares for an aging parent with respect and understanding. Such love endures the rejection of a teenager without resentment, and stands by to encourage—but not rescue—a child suffering the consequences of a bad decision. Godlike love says: "I will humbly put aside my own needs and desires to work for your good." It is the love whose words and deeds most closely resemble the words of Christ. That is why authentic Christlike love is often sacrificial. It is not a "what's-in-it-for-me?" love, but rather a "what-can-I-give?" love.

Love with Your Mind, Heart, and Will

While the gift of willed love is an expression of Christlike love, this does not mean that emotional love is unnecessary or frivolous. Ordinarily, people do not even make a distinction between the emotion or feeling of love and a willed act of love. We tend to identify all love with the "feeling" of love. That is because we react as a total human being united in body and soul, emotion, intellect, and will, and that is good. Even our love for God should encompass both the emotions and will as Christ taught: "[Y]ou shall love the Lord your God with all your heart, and with all your soul, and with all your mind, and with all your strength…[and] your neighbor as yourself" (Mark 12:30-31).

In fact, it is this union of emotional and willed love that activates an experience of "transfiguration," not unlike that of the three apostles who were overcome with joy as they experienced the glorified Christ on Mount Tabor. We, like them, are overwhelmed at times with the goodness of another and drawn by desire to love completely, sacrificially, with utter joy; to make ourselves a gift for the other. When this gift of self is returned by the one we love, it is a mutual "gift-love."

Responding to God's call to love with a generous giving of self is our only possibility for real happiness, joy, and deep abiding peace in this life. Like a magnet, love is the force pulling us toward God, in whom alone we can be fully satisfied: "You have made us for yourself, O Lord, and our hearts are restless until they rest in you" (Saint Augustine, *Confessions,* 1.1).

REMEMBER:

The whole purpose of generous, mutual gift-love is to unite us with the God who made us out of love. How can men and women become responsible lovers, whose sexual love is a fully human love?

Through a Virtuous Life

Finally, beloved, whatever is true,
whatever is honorable, whatever is just,
whatever is pure, whatever is pleasing,
whatever is commendable, if there is any
excellence and if there is anything worthy
of praise, think about these things.

PHILIPPIANS 4:8

We are like travelers en route to God. We need more than a desire and a willingness to get to our destination. There is much—both within us and without us—that frustrates our desire and willingness to love: our own weaknesses, confused reasoning, and personal adversities in life which can undermine our faith and hope. We need "strategies of love"! We call these strategies virtues. The virtues give our love shape and meaning, and make us morally ingenious and skillful.

We Become Who We Want to Be

We move toward wholeness and holiness through practicing virtuous acts of mind, heart, and will that gradually shape us into the greatness we are called to become. We have the capacity to become extremely good, noble, and beautiful, but we also have the freedom to destroy our good and thus become corrupt. In this earthly life, we stand poised between the possibility for greatness or awfulness, saint or sinner. Embracing virtues make us morally exquisite, while practicing vices make us morally flawed and ultimately destroy what God intends for us.

Vice Diminishes, Virtue Enhances Our Humanity

We all know persons who grace our lives by their compassion, integrity, courage, patience, wisdom, and honor, and we also know persons who assault us with their greed, lust, dishonesty, cowardice, selfishness, impatience, or arrogance. While vice perverts what our human nature was meant to achieve, the more we grow in virtue, the more genuinely human and holy we become.

We Become Virtuous Persons

A virtue is more than a nice thought or correct perspective on life. Virtues reside in personal actions. A virtue is an attitude, disposition, or habit that guides our actions toward what is good. Directed by reason and will, repeated acts of virtue will make us attain a quality of character: We become virtuous persons. At first, we are clumsy and inept at developing a virtue, but, over time, the virtue becomes second nature to us. Through continuous acts of kindness and forgiveness, we become kind and forgiving persons. We become what we most consistently do.

Virtues Are More than Pleasant Habits

With God's grace, natural virtues can be transformed into supernatural virtues which gently guide our steps along the path to God. Over time, our "habitual" moral goodness helps make our steps surer in their placement and lighter in effort. We are transformed into persons who predictably and delightfully do good. According to Thomas Aquinas, natural moral goodness needs the grace of God to become habitual moral goodness.

Falling into Vice Is as Easy as Taking a Wrong Turn

Sadly, it is all too easy to stray from the moral path to God; it is so easy to adopt patterns of behavior—perhaps insignificant at first—that over time lead us far away from where we ought or want to be. To end up someone other than who God intended us to be is not difficult or rare. Vices are habits too often ingrained:

gossiping, laziness, cheating, being quick-tempered, eating or drinking too much. Developing virtue often begins with uprooting vice and its power over our life.

Virtue Takes
Hard Work and Vigilance

Most often, we are not a freshly tilled field ready and eager for the planting of seeds of virtue to take root and blossom. We can be like hardened soil with weeds entrenched, requiring the difficult task of uprooting the weeds, tilling the soil to make it ready to plant the seeds of virtue. For these to take root in us—and for the tender shoots to grow—they must be nurtured, fed, and protected so they can become sturdy, healthy, blossom, and bear fruit. The weeds can grow back quickly and easily choke out the young shoots of virtue. By daily vigilance and attention to the growth of virtue, the harvest will bring mature fruit, sweet and abundant.

"Virtuoso"—An Expert at Virtue

The task of the moral life is to become so familiar with good that one becomes "a virtuoso": a person eloquent with goodness. Only through God's grace can the virtues transform us and bring us closer to divine union. What becomes of us is in our hands and God's graceful plan. It takes the full devotion of our energy and the grace of God to be good, noble, and beautiful. Only through God's grace can the virtues transform us wayfarers, and bring us closer to our goal: union with God.

REMEMBER:

Becoming virtuous helps us toward becoming a real lover of God and others.

Shaped by the Virtue of Charity

[I]f I have all faith, so as to remove
mountains, but do not
have love, I am nothing.

<small>1 Corinthians 13:2</small>

Any virtue will be hollow or short-lived if it
isn't guided by charity and directed toward a
wholehearted love of God. When charity—that
passionate and heartfelt love of God—is the
intention of our life, then all virtues are born of
charity and work for the sake of charity. Charity
is the mother of all virtue, "which binds everything together in perfect harmony" (Colossians
3:14). It "is the *form of the virtues;* it articulates
and orders them among themselves; it is the
source and the goal of their Christian practice.
Charity upholds and purifies our human ability to love, and raises it to the supernatural perfection of divine love" (CCC 1827).

Charity Is Love That Is Other-Directed

Charity is love that fully acknowledges the dignity and worth of each person as an image in the likeness of God. Charity is "unreasonable" love. We respond and act in a loving way not just in the face of a person with a few irritating habits, but also to those who hurt, offend, or even repulse us. Charity is love that completely respects and accepts the "otherness" of the loved one, including his or her faults and limitations. Charity is a conscious, free, fully human act of love that refrains from doing anything that would harm the other physically, emotionally, or spiritually. When we love with genuine charity, we passionately work to do everything in our power to always act in the best interest of the other. Therefore, Paul can say:

*Love is patient...kind...not envious or
boastful or arrogant or rude. It does
not insist on its own way; it is not irritable
or resentful; it does not rejoice in
wrongdoing, but rejoices in the truth. It
bears all things, believes all things, hopes
all things, endures all things.*

(1 CORINTHIANS 13:3-7)

Charity Is the Soul of Holiness

"Charity is the soul of the holiness to which all are called: it 'governs, shapes, and perfects all the means of sanctification'" (CCC 826). Our life begun in grace is a call to glory. Through a virtuous life directed by charity we find life in Christ.

The Source of Virtuous Living

Each virtue is derived from the four cardinal virtues. If an act is virtuous, we should be able to look at it from different angles and see in it prudence, justice, temperance, and courage. What does a virtue look like if it is not rooted in love? Prudence or right judgment becomes clever, cunning, crafty, shrewd, savvy. Justice becomes fair, lacking in compassion or understanding, and giving only what is "due." Temperance becomes prudery, and fortitude or courage is translated into risk taking.

Prudence, right judgment or moral wisdom, is primary because virtue is never a rote or mechanical way of behaving, but a moral skill of discernment as to what is good and of how it can be carried out. Prudence gives an ingenuity to our love, and it takes a "moral artistry" to be prudent.

Justice is doing what needs to be done once prudence determines what is morally right. If prudence is right judgment, then justice is right action. In the service of love, justice ensures that the most loving action will be taken.

Courage keeps us steadfast when we are discouraged or confronted with adversity that may tempt us to relinquish what is right. Courage enables us to endure in times of hardship and not be deterred from acting out of love because of our own fear or inadequacy.

Temperance directs our emotions when they could otherwise become so powerful as to make us rash or careless, or so listless that we become apathetic and don't want to do anything at all. Temperance "tempers" our emotions, either up or down, and channels our desires to the service of love.

REMEMBER:

All virtue shaped by charity is authentic virtue. Any virtue not grounded in love may be hollow, empty, and in vain.

We Then Understand Chastity...

*Do you not know that your bodies are members of Christ?
...therefore glorify God in your body.*
1 CORINTHIANS 6:15,20

Chastity Flows from Prudence

Chastity also bears the marks of the four cardinal virtues. First, chastity flows from prudence because it is a virtue that is not shortsighted, but is visionary because it sees the truth of the mystery of being created in God's image as a sexual person in both body and spirit. Chastity is to revere what God has done in creating us sexual persons.

Chastity Flows from Justice

Next, chastity seeks to act in a way that respects our sexual powers with their awesome potential to bond a relationship in love, and to give life to a new and unique person, destined to live for all eternity. The virtue of chastity enables us to relate to each person we meet as a wonderful creature of God, made for his or her own sake and deserving to be loved as an image of God. Chastity says *yes* to the goodness of our sexuality, and makes it possible for us to become sexual persons capable of loving as Christ loves.

Chastity Flows from Temperance

Chastity does not suppress our sexual desire, but gradually transforms, intensifies, and orients our sexual desire and energy into loving actions and creative pursuits. Temperance is mastery of oneself for the purpose of giving of oneself. Chastity recognizes and affirms sexual intercourse as an integral part of the mutual and generous "gift-love" between husband and wife. Rather than our sexual desire and passion enslaving and degrading our dignity as human persons, chastity frees us from selfishness and aggression, and gives us the spiritual power to love with true charity.

Chastity Flows from Courage

Chastity makes it possible for us to stand our ground in the face of repeated temptation to misdirected sexual behavior, or thoughts and words unworthy of us. The virtue of chastity keeps us strong when passions might weaken us, or when we encounter temptations outside our self to act on our sexual desires in an unloving or shortsighted way. To live chastely requires a heroic effort in a climate which, most often, ignores that chastity is a virtue.

Chastity, the "Sentry" of Shame

Thomas Aquinas calls sensitivity to shame "a healthy fear of being inglorious," and says it is a valuable moral quality in developing virtue. The great difficulty with respect to developing the virtue of chastity is that shame has been divorced from unchaste, intemperate, or ungodly expression of sexual behavior in today's cultural environment.

The "sentry" of shame—guarding our dignity and moral integrity—has abandoned the gate of sexual conduct and the way we express our sexual desire. When we are numb or deadened to what debases us, we make wide open the opportunity for selfishness and the misuse of our sexual powers, which is called lust. We can become quite shameless about it. We can even become brazen about it, and end up refusing the opportunity for grace and redemption.

A chaste approach to life keeps that "sentry" of shame alert so as to uphold our dignity, moral integrity, and openness to God's grace and redemption. Chastity viewed from all angles reflects the four cardinal virtues and, like those, accomplishes good when directed by charity.

Chastity Without Charity Is Counterfeit

Chastity without love is superficial. It is a right and good act deprived of its power to change and transform us into the person God is calling each of us to be. Chastity is a "spiritual power capable of defending love from the perils of selfishness and aggressiveness and able to advance it towards its full realization" (John Paul II, *Familiaris Consortio,* 33).

Chastity shaped by love makes us vividly aware that our sexual powers are an incredible gift. Living chastely makes it possible for us to extend God's life-giving love to others, whether it be channeling our sexual desire into a pure love for many others with an undivided heart or transforming the sexual act into its greatest potential: to be our most "godlike" in the total self-gift to one another in an openness to the creation of new life.

...And Why Chastity Reveals the Mystery of Love in Everyone

As many of you as were baptized into Christ have clothed yourselves with Christ.

GALATIANS 3:27

Because we are sexual persons from birth to death, it follows that chastity is a virtue for *everyone* at every age or stage of life: young, middle-aged, old, married and unmarried, male and female. God calls us to daily affirm the truth, beauty, and goodness of our human sexuality. It is a lifelong way of thinking and acting that is in accord with the truth of human and divine love—to live lives of holiness.

An Apprenticeship for Marriage

For persons preparing for marriage, living the virtue of chastity is an apprenticeship in fidelity. A chaste life allows each individual sexual person to grow toward the fullest integration of his or her emotions, intellect, creativity, and ultimate call to love wholeheartedly in true friendship.

Pursuing purity of mind, body, and soul during this apprenticeship allows each person to discover the beauty, goodness and dignity of him or herself. This makes it possible for each to be truly a gift of self for the other in marriage.

Unchastity Leads to Sexual Disintegration

Misdirection of our sexual desire into painful unchaste experiences inhibits or blocks our ability to develop ourselves as fully sexual persons, diminishes our dignity, and tarnishes the beauty of our gifts. Misdirection of our sexual desires leads to sexual disintegration.

In spite of this truth, however, we live in a culture that encourages us to act on any and all of our sexual desires, and even to separate them from the life-giving power of love. These influences can lead those preparing for marriage to painful unchaste experiences with the consequence of retarding growth toward sexual wholeness. Even so, with a sincere desire to be reconciled with God and the truth of oneself, we can reaffirm the truth of our sexuality and rededicate ourselves to live that truth with a chaste mind and heart. Christ wants nothing less than for each person to know and experience the fullness of life in him.

Chastity in Marriage Enables the Gift of Self

An atmosphere of chastity in marriage secures mutual respect and fidelity between the spouses. Chastity enables husband and wife to continually be a "sincere gift of self" (*Gaudium et Spes,* 24). Through the union of their bodies and souls in the act of sexual intercourse, a husband and wife reaffirm their bond of love with one another and receive new life as a gift of their married love.

For married persons, chastity is at the service of the spouses' love for one another and the future of the family. Chastity informed by charity safeguards the integrity of the marital bond and protects the children's right to experience a mother and father who love each other and a family life characterized by unity and faithfulness.

The Family Is First in Living and Teaching Chastity

The family, rightly called by the Church "the domestic church," is the first community in which each child will learn the true meaning of life and love. Married persons also fall short of their call to live chastely and to love exclusively, to respect the other for his or her self, and to keep each act of intercourse open to new life. But God loves the family, is rich in mercy and compassion, and desires only that we seek—and live in—reconciliation.

Chastity in the Celibate State Aids an Undivided Heart

For those whose vocational call is to a committed or vowed celibate state in life, chastity can be a freeing, all-encompassing love of God and all others with an undivided heart. Chastity rooted in celibate charity facilitates a love that bears a strong witness to the presence of God's reign in this world.

Those who respond generously to God's call to a celibate way of life face the greatest challenge in today's culture in that they aren't encouraged to see themselves as fully sexual persons, nor are they viewed as able to be wholly sexual human beings. Because the truth about the supernatural meaning of our sexual nature has been widely rejected, the truth about the proper nature of being a fully loving sexual person apart from availing onself to the act of intercourse is incomprehensible to many.

Chastity enables a person called to express the gift of celibacy—whether vowed or not—to develop as a fully sexual person who channels sexual desire into creative and loving pursuits. When informed by charity, a chaste attitude frees all of us from self-centeredness, but it does not repress the longing to love and be loved. By developing the capacity for comprehensively loving others—a love of the heart and the will—one is able to pour out to God and others a warm, generous, and outgoing love.

Made to Love Chastely

The story of human life comes full circle. We begin by being created out of love, and we end in a longing to be finally reunited with the God whose love made us. What comes in-between is the Christian life. The Christian life calls each of us to be holy. As Christians, we believe that a life of virtue directed by love is the only source of true joy and peace, simply because it is the only path to God. Virtues, such as chastity, can transform our humanness into godliness. We grow in virtue through grace, knowledge, deliberate actions, and perseverance.

We Are Not Alone in Our Pursuit of Holiness

It is important to know that, no matter how good and holy we strive to become, we will never merit God. At its depths, our attempts to love is a continual cry to God to do for us what we cannot do for ourselves. The outpouring of God's grace in our hearts completes what our virtues alone can never achieve.

At exactly the point where virtue can do no more, we are blessed by God with the gift of love poured out in the Holy Spirit given to us. Our journey is sustained and directed by the Spirit taking hold of us. Dwelling freely in us, the Holy Spirit transforms our very being by sanctifying us, i.e., making us holy.

> *Just as the branch cannot bear*
> *fruit by itself unless it abides in the vine,*
> *neither can you unless you abide in me.*
> *I am the vine, you are the branches.*
> *Those who abide in me and I in them*
> *bear much fruit, because apart from*
> *me you can do nothing.*
>
> JOHN 15:4-5

We are not independent operators; we are many branches connected to a single vine bearing the fruits of the Holy Spirit to build up the entire Body of Christ. Our desire to live a chaste life—our pursuit of holiness—contributes to the holiness of others.

We Are in Good Company

If we let go of our struggles and attempts to be holy, the whole Body of Christ is affected. But when we bind ourselves to the communion of saints through prayer, good works, reconciliation, and seeing our pain as part of the sufferings of Christ, grace flows, not only through ourselves but through the whole community: "Each one sustains the rest and the rest sustains each other" (Saint Gregory the Great, *Homilies on Ezekiel*, 2,1,5). God's promise of total restoration is then realized, bringing us healing, wholeness, happiness, and peace. In the end, we will come to know the glory we are called to. Only then are we finally at peace, because we are at rest in God.

REMEMBER:

The virtue of chastity is for everyone because it maintains the integrity of our sexuality and safeguards the powers of life and love placed in us. For everyone chastity is a gift, a grace, and the fruit of spiritual effort.

...And Why Chastity Preserves the Gift of Self

How do we *live* the virtue of chastity? Through a continual openness to the presence of Christ—the Word made flesh—who is always with us. This is not easy, but it is our call as human and sexual persons. God never asks us to do anything without giving us the power to do it: "I can do all things through him who strengthens me" (Philippians 4:13).

Here is a self-evaluation checklist that may make practical the meaning of chastity. It can be used by anyone at any stage or in any state of life, because chastity is for everyone.

* Do I think of myself as being totally sexual and work on a personal identity that is strong in all dimensions: Spiritual, Physical, Intellectual, Creative, Emotional (SPICE)?

- Am I forming friendships with persons that respect the dignity and "genius" of their masculinity/femininity?
- Do I think and speak positively about gender equality and differences?
- Am I in the habit of seeking out positive media outlets, books, and magazines that encourage virtuous, respectful treatment of sex, marriage, relationships?
- Am I willing to turn off music, videos, TV, or Internet sites that trivialize sex, entice one into sexual fantasy, or feed impure curiosity about sexual behavior?
- Do I avoid listening to or discussing putdowns on sexual topics, whether jokes, vulgarity, stories, or comments about others?
- Am I always dressed in a way that invites someone to want to get to know me instead of seeing me as an object of sensual pleasure?
- Do I seek friendships or relationships that

will support my desire to be chaste amidst a sexually provocative culture?

- Can I insist on my right to be different by my unwavering commitment to modesty in thought, word, and action?
- Am I committed to praying daily for God's grace to sustain me and others in living chastity, especially for those in my family, my friends, my coworkers, and in my social life?
- Do I ask God's forgiveness when I sin against chastity, receive mercy gratefully, and try again to re-commit to chaste living?
- Am I steadfast in my pursuit of a virtuous life, making chastity a lifelong goal to keep sex sacred?
- Do I avoid engaging in behavior that is sexually arousing and may lead to sexual intercourse outside of marriage?
- Have I made a habit of supporting the belief that sexual intercourse is a wonderful gift of married love, and that children are the blessing of that love?

Discipline yourselves, keep alert. Like a roaring lion your adversary the devil prowls around, looking for someone to devour. Resist him, steadfast in your faith, for you know that your brothers and sisters in all the world are undergoing the same kinds of suffering. And after you have suffered for a little while, the God of all grace, who has called you to his eternal glory in Christ, will himself restore, support, strengthen, and establish you. To him be the power forever and ever. Amen

1 PETER 5:8-11